Vietnamese Girls

Hot Sexy Vietnamese Lingerie Girls Models Pictures

By **PHOTO ART LOVER**

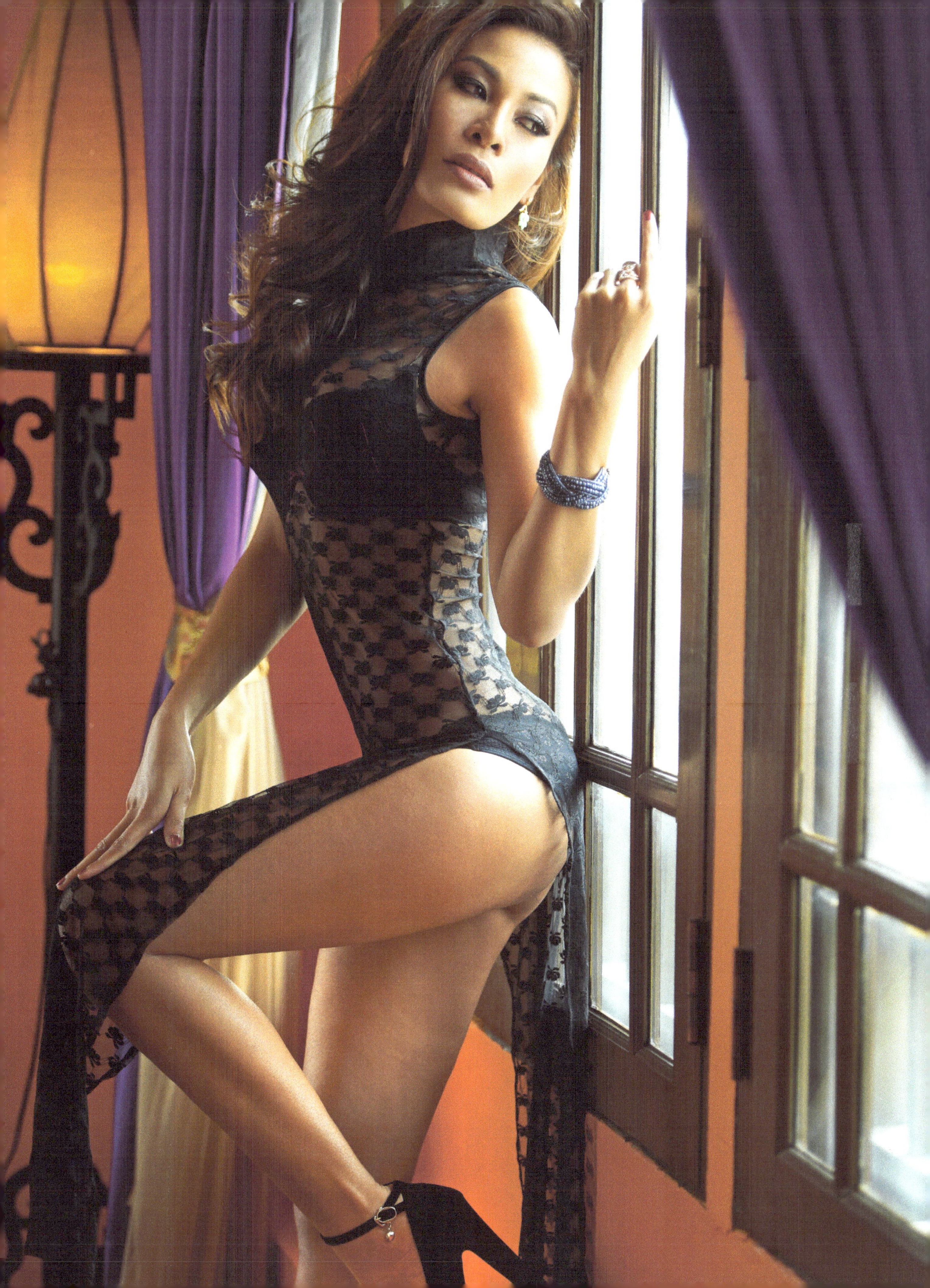

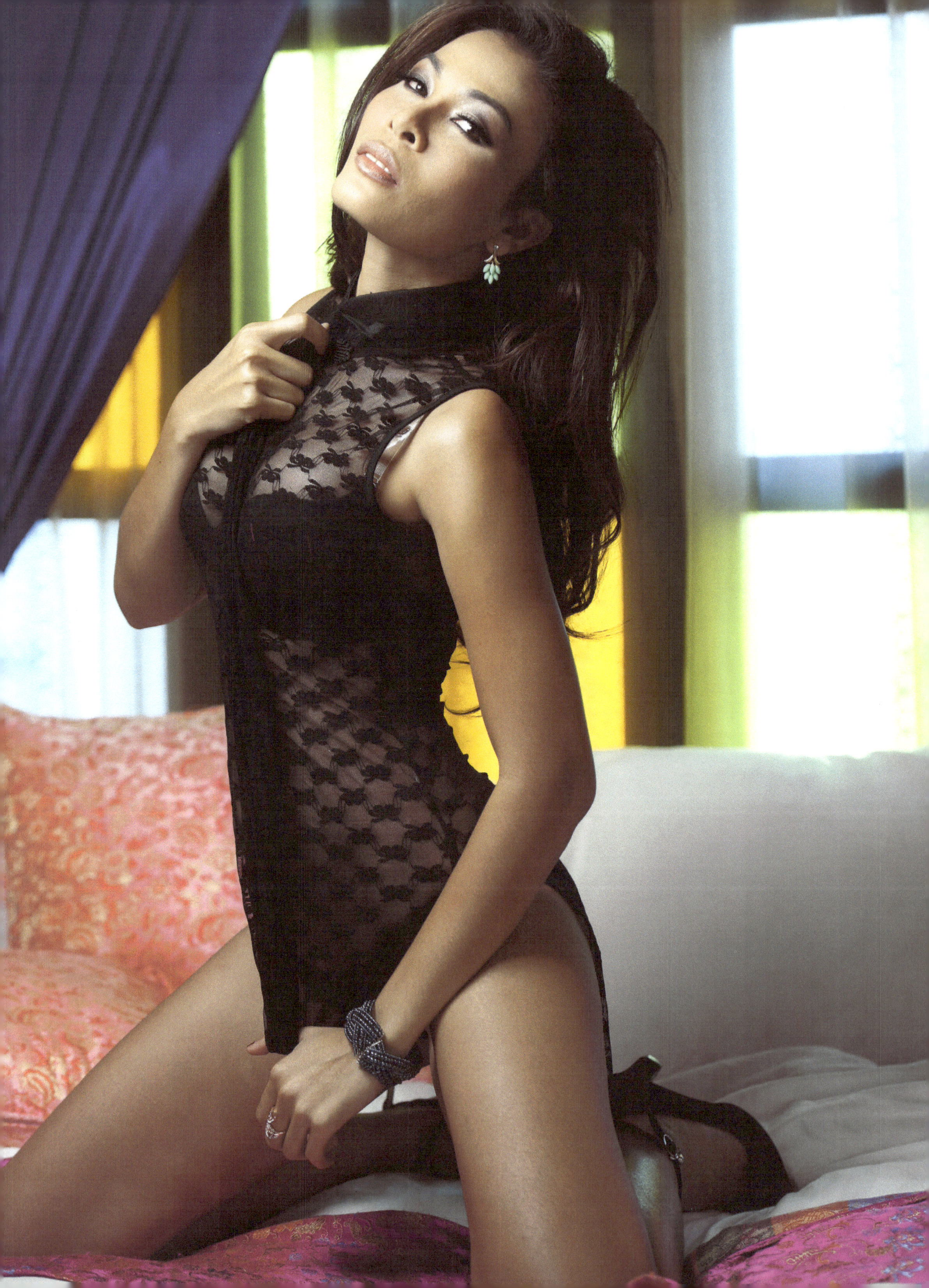

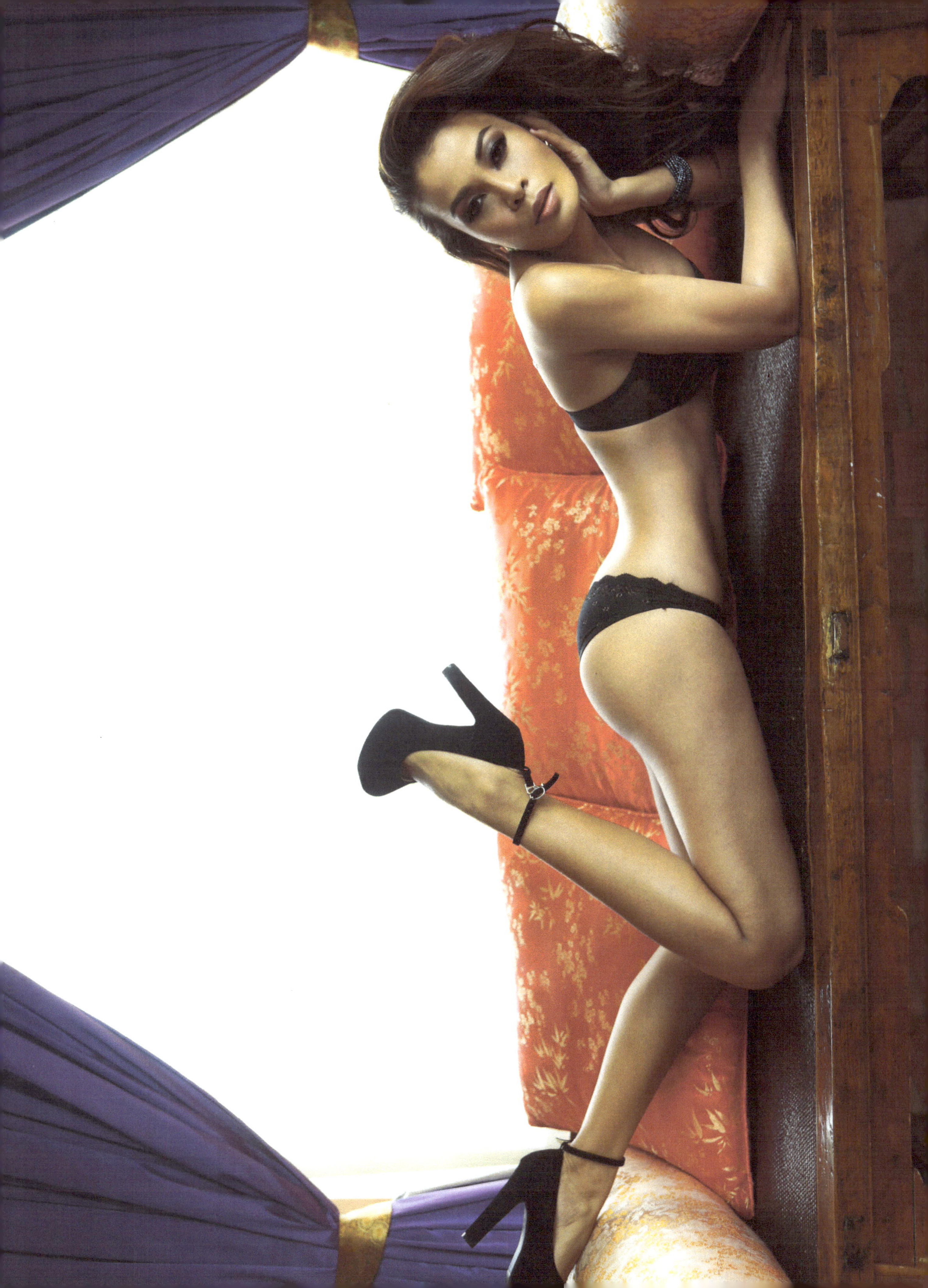

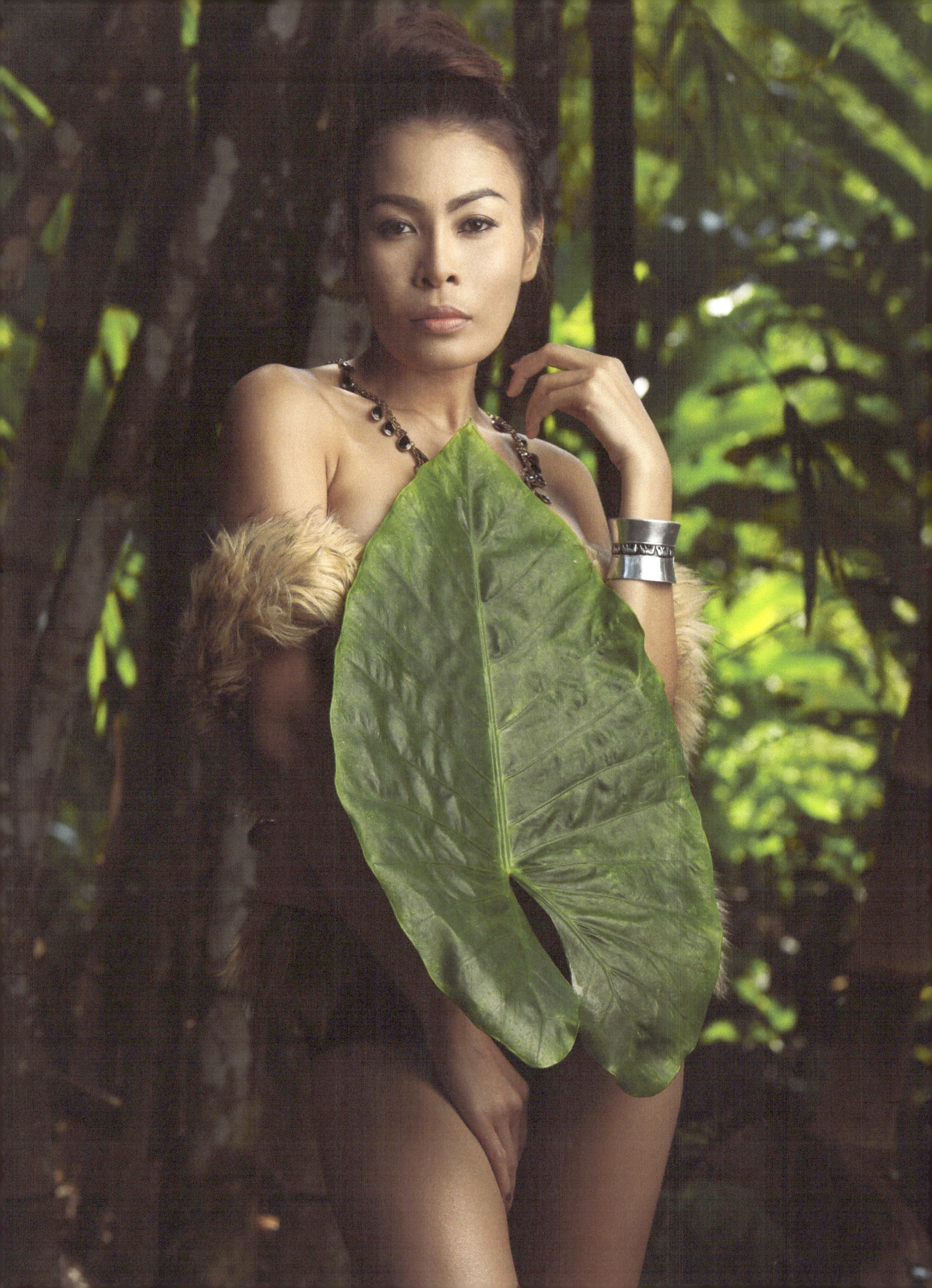

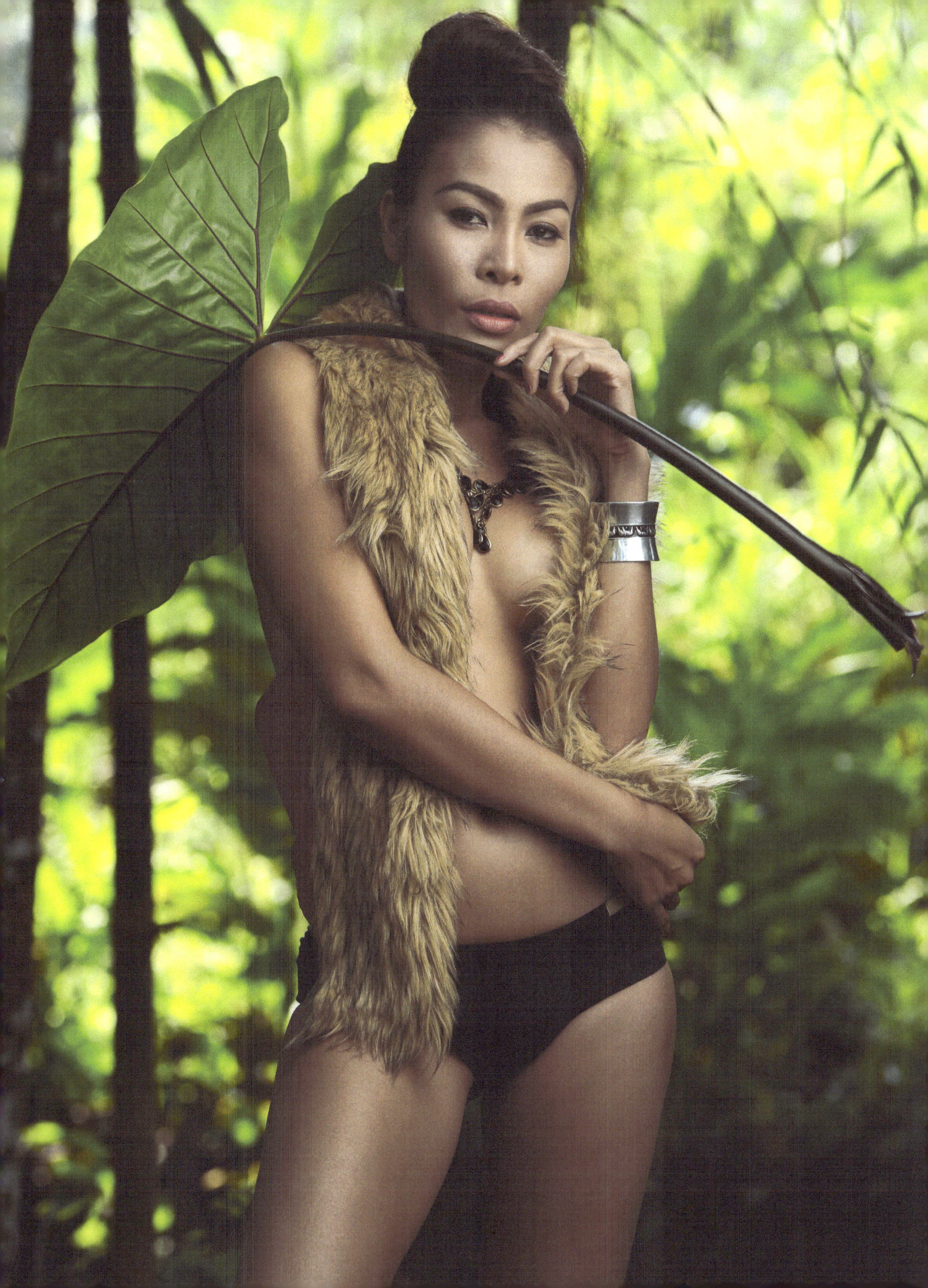

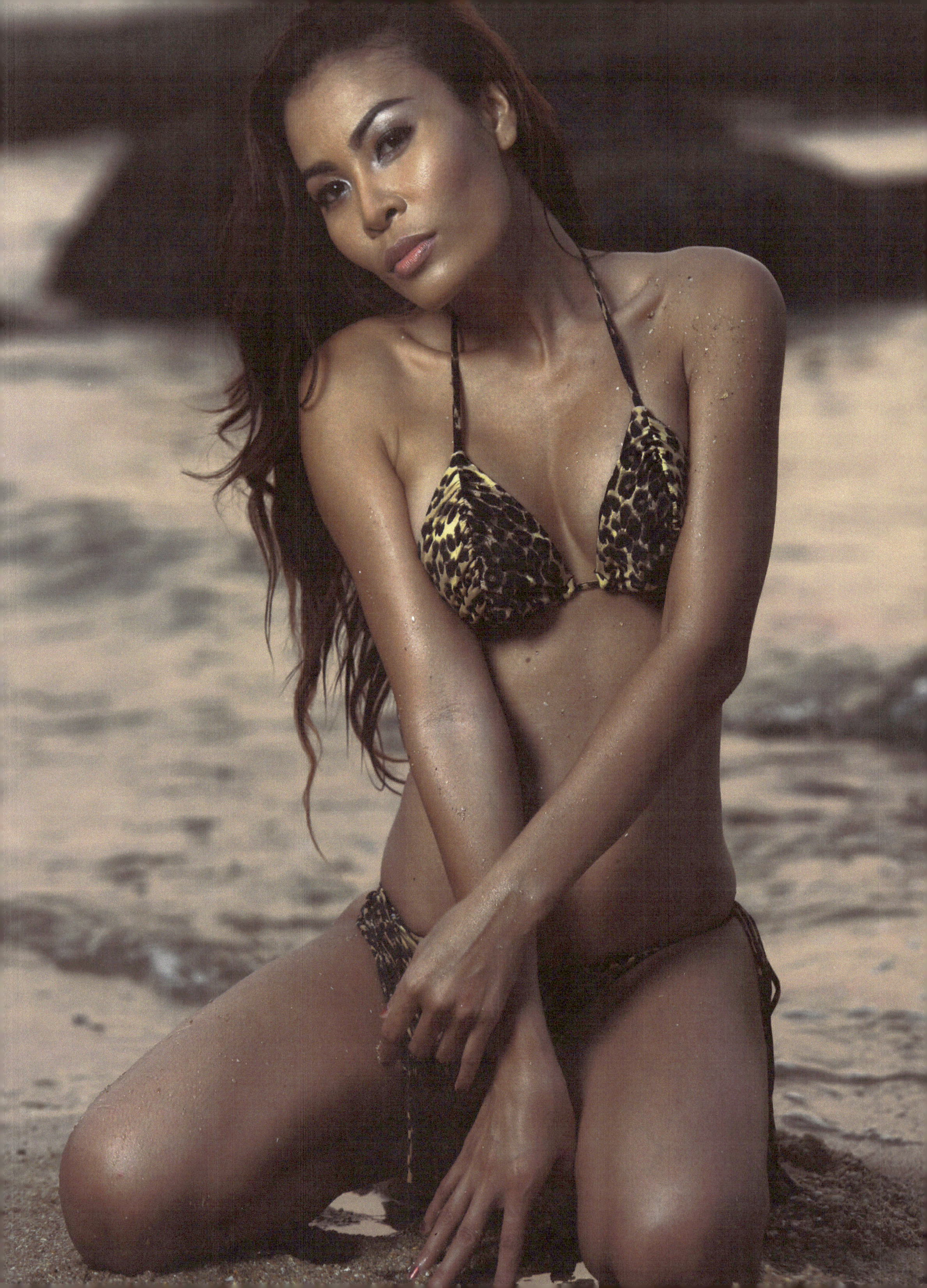

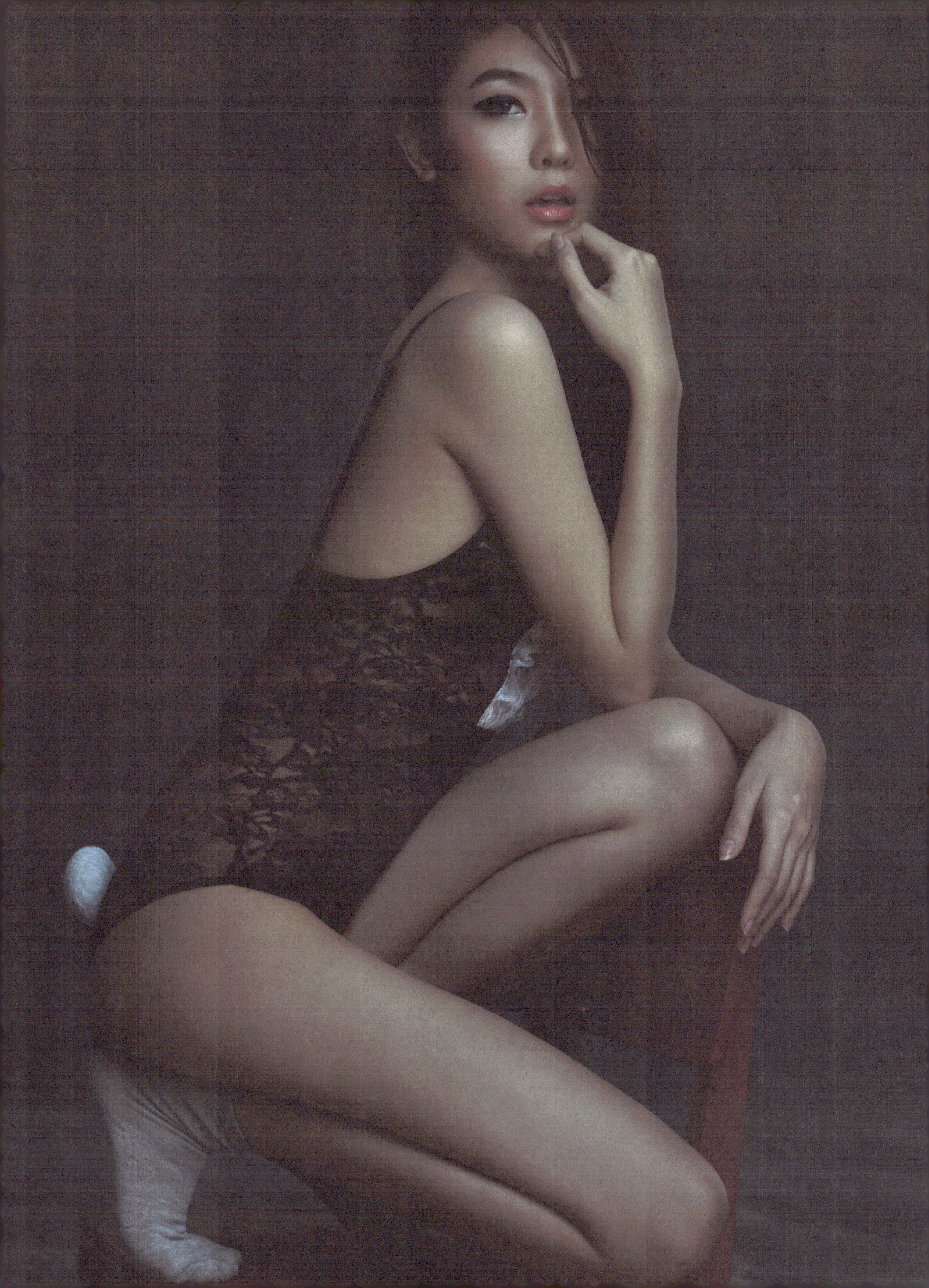

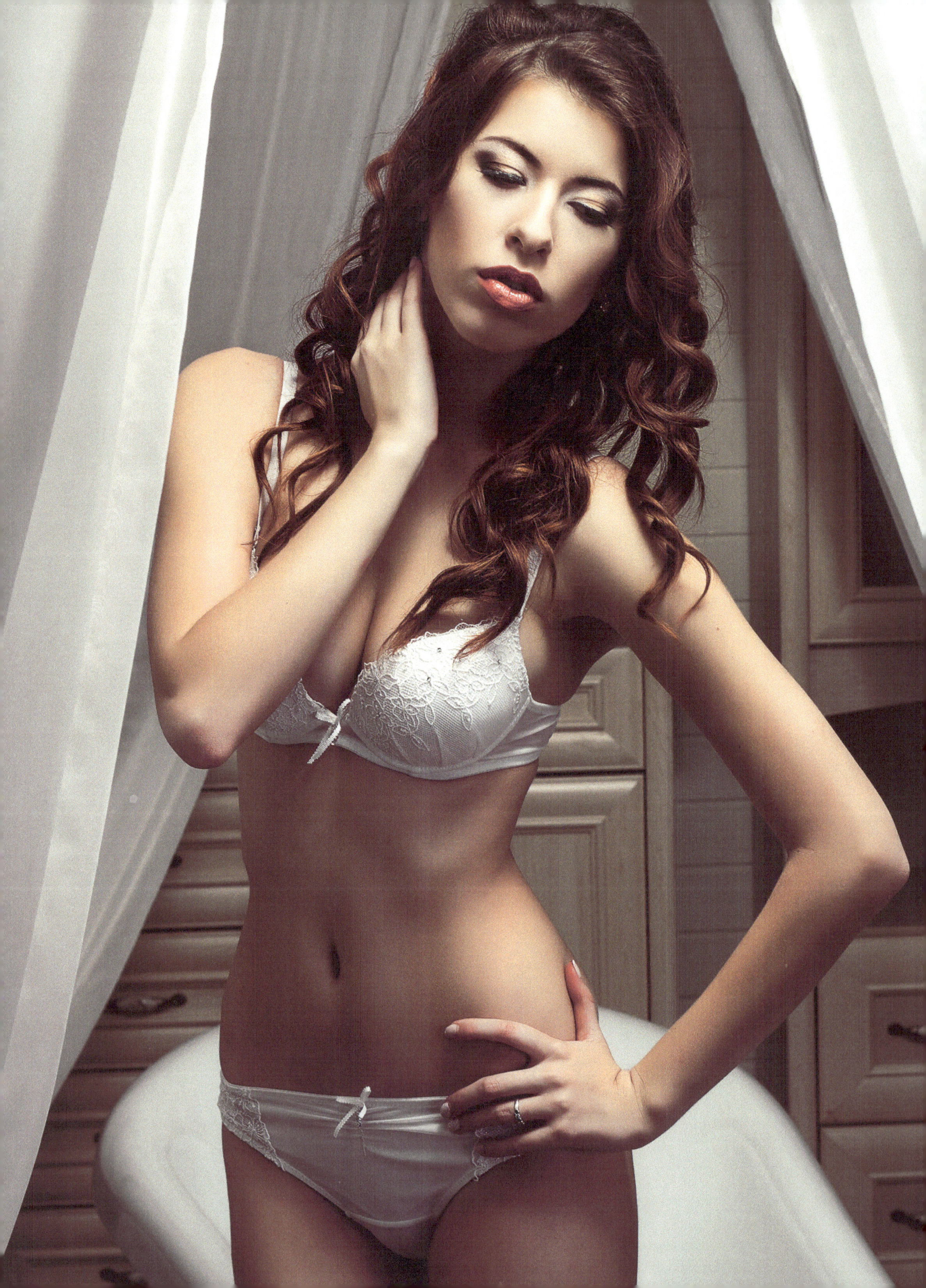

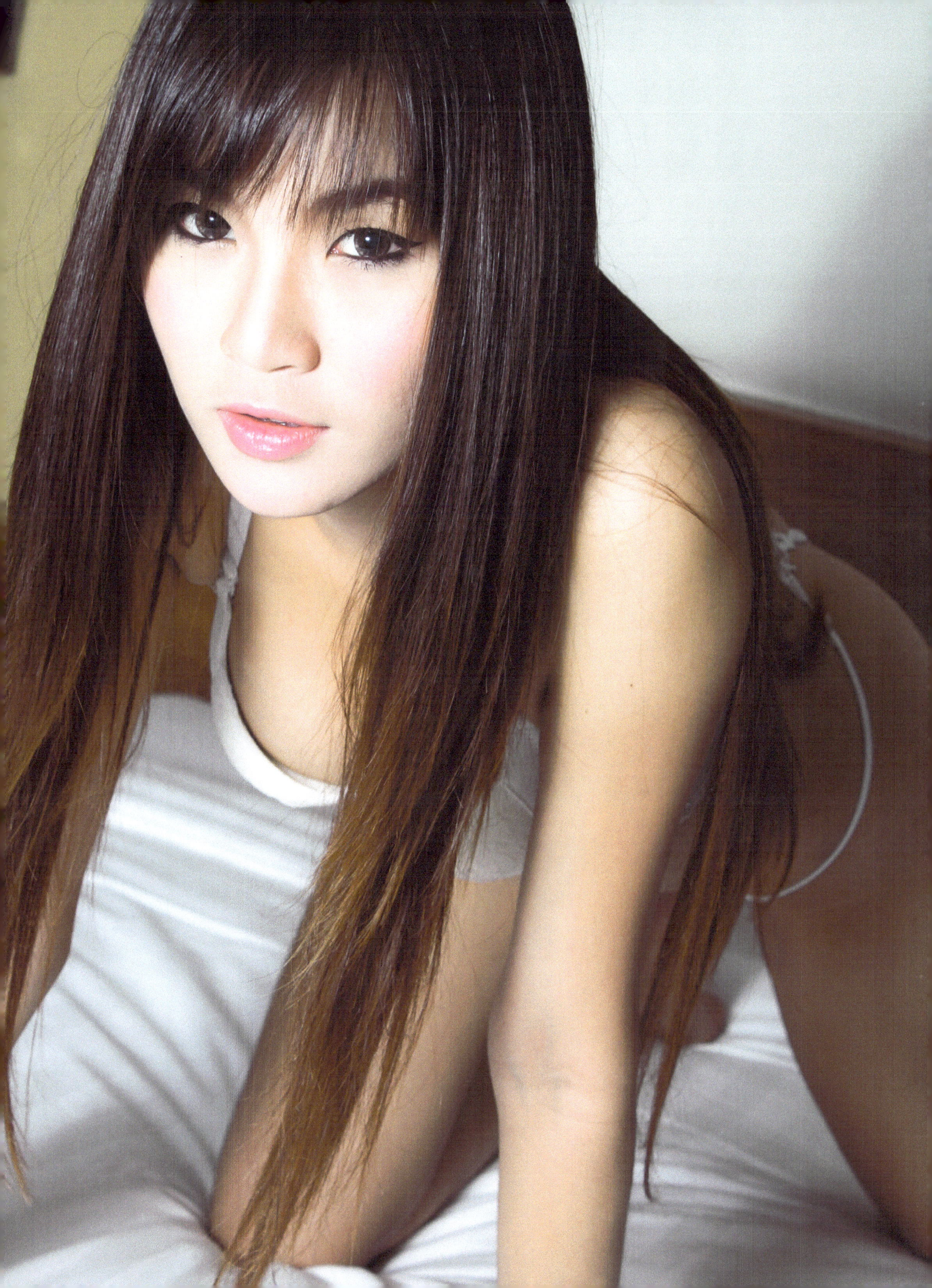

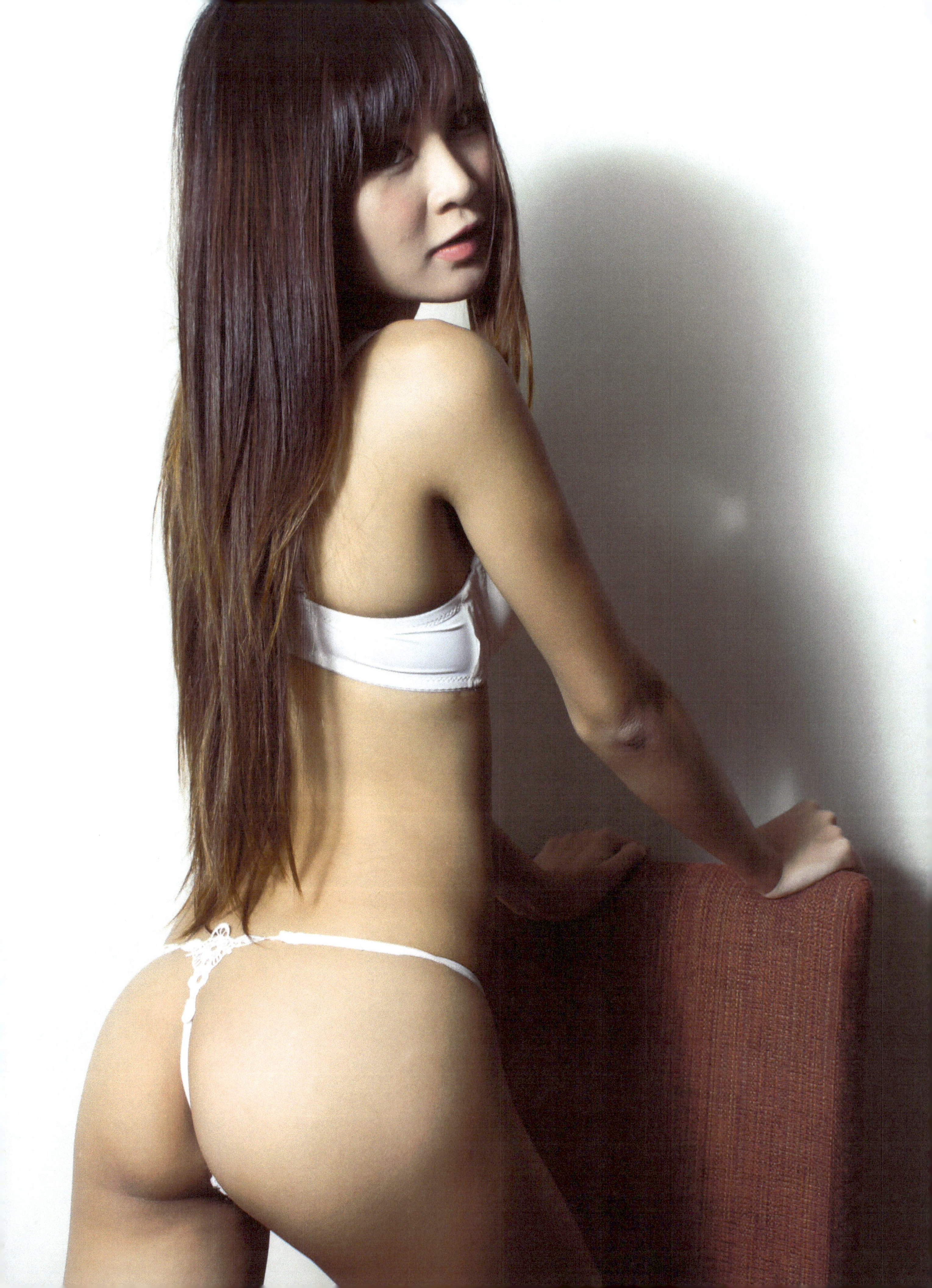

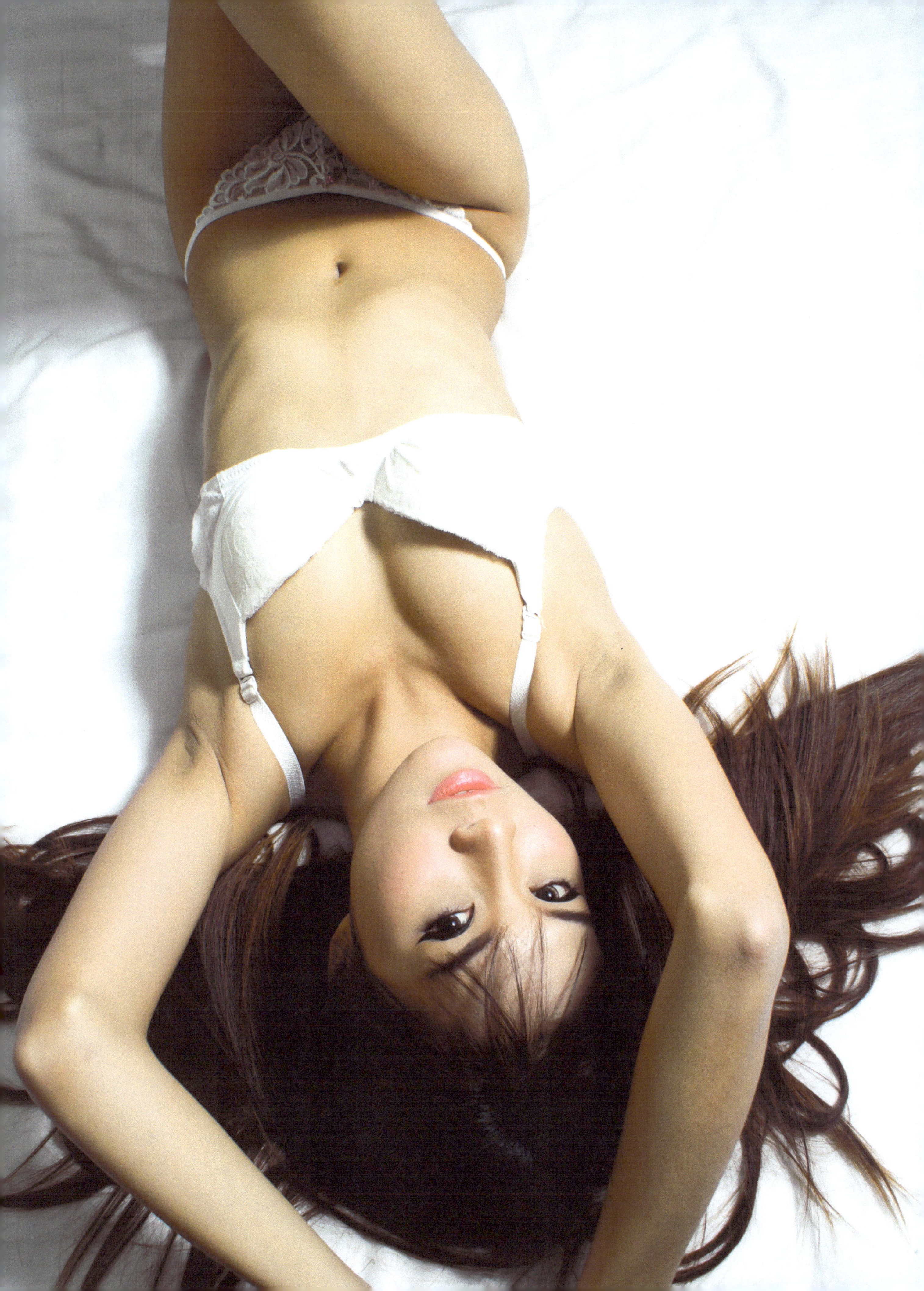

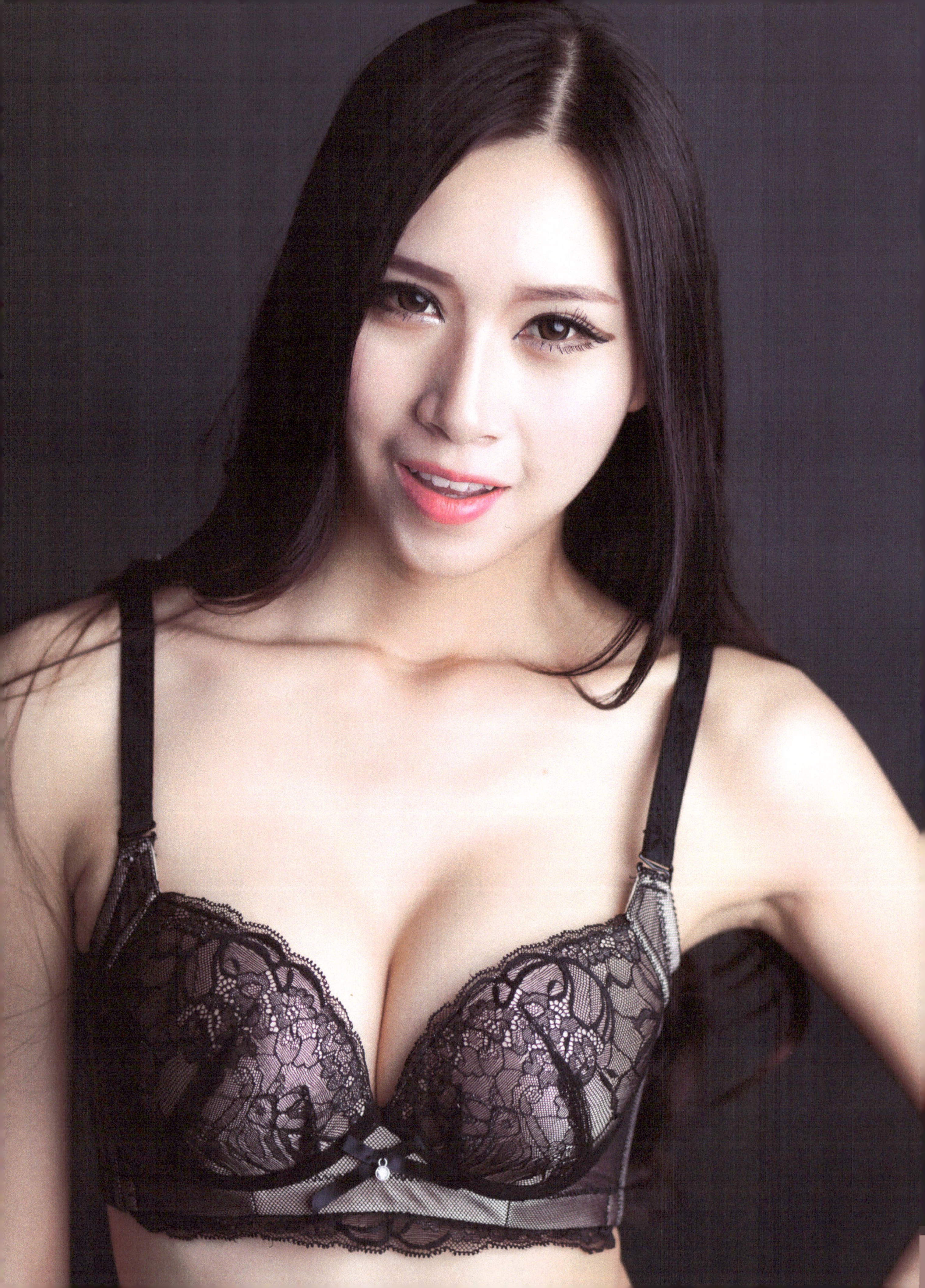

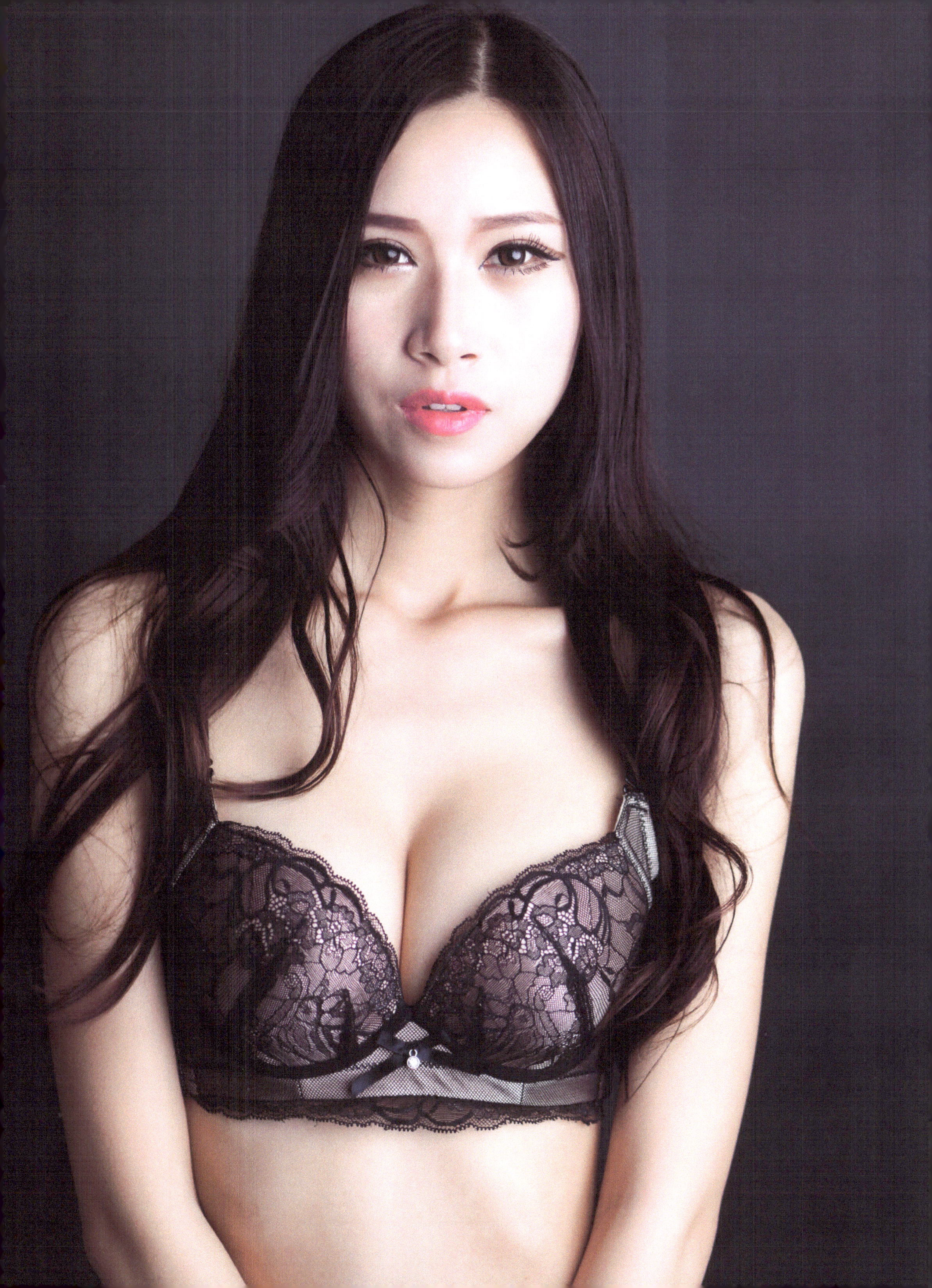

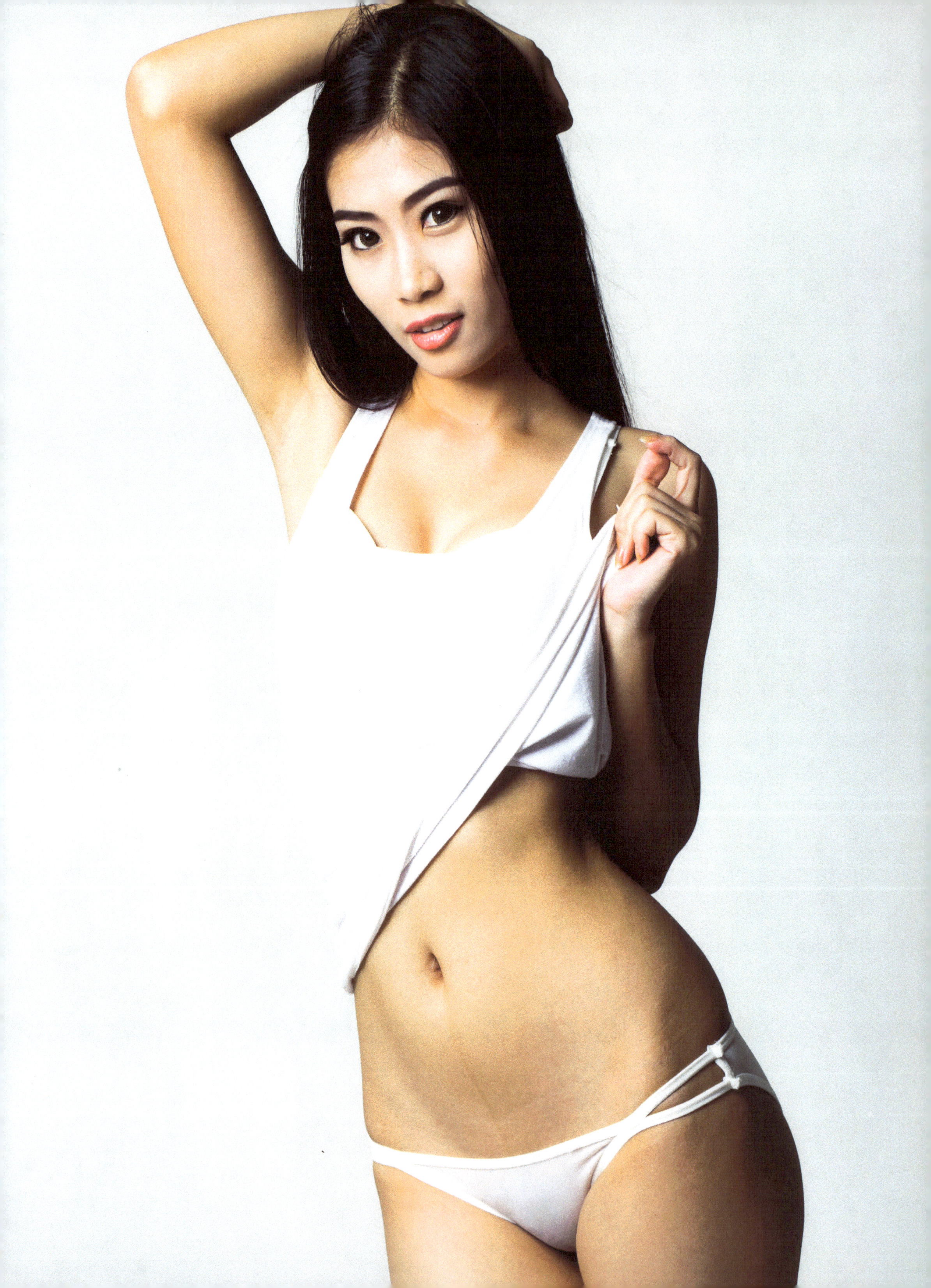

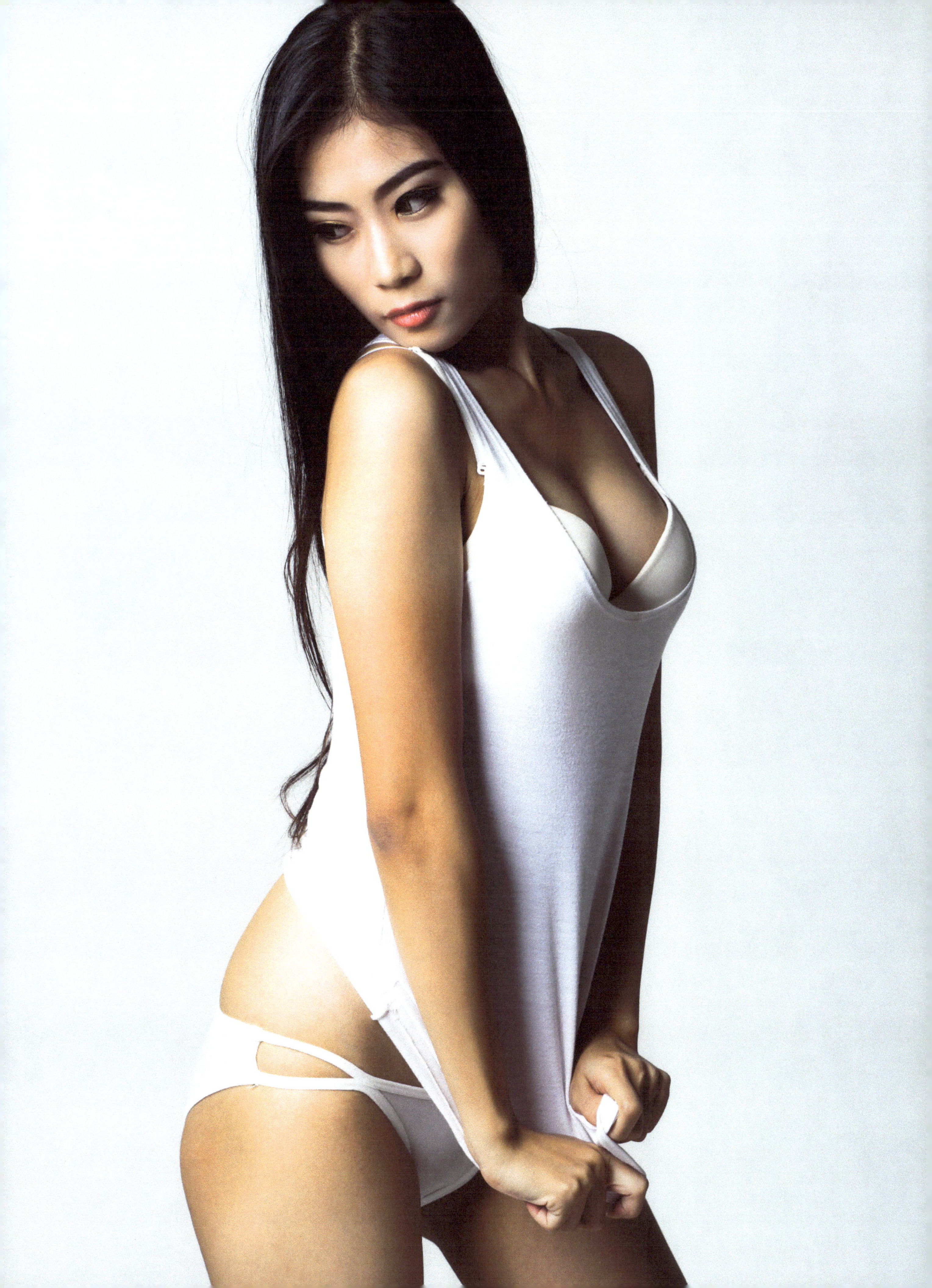

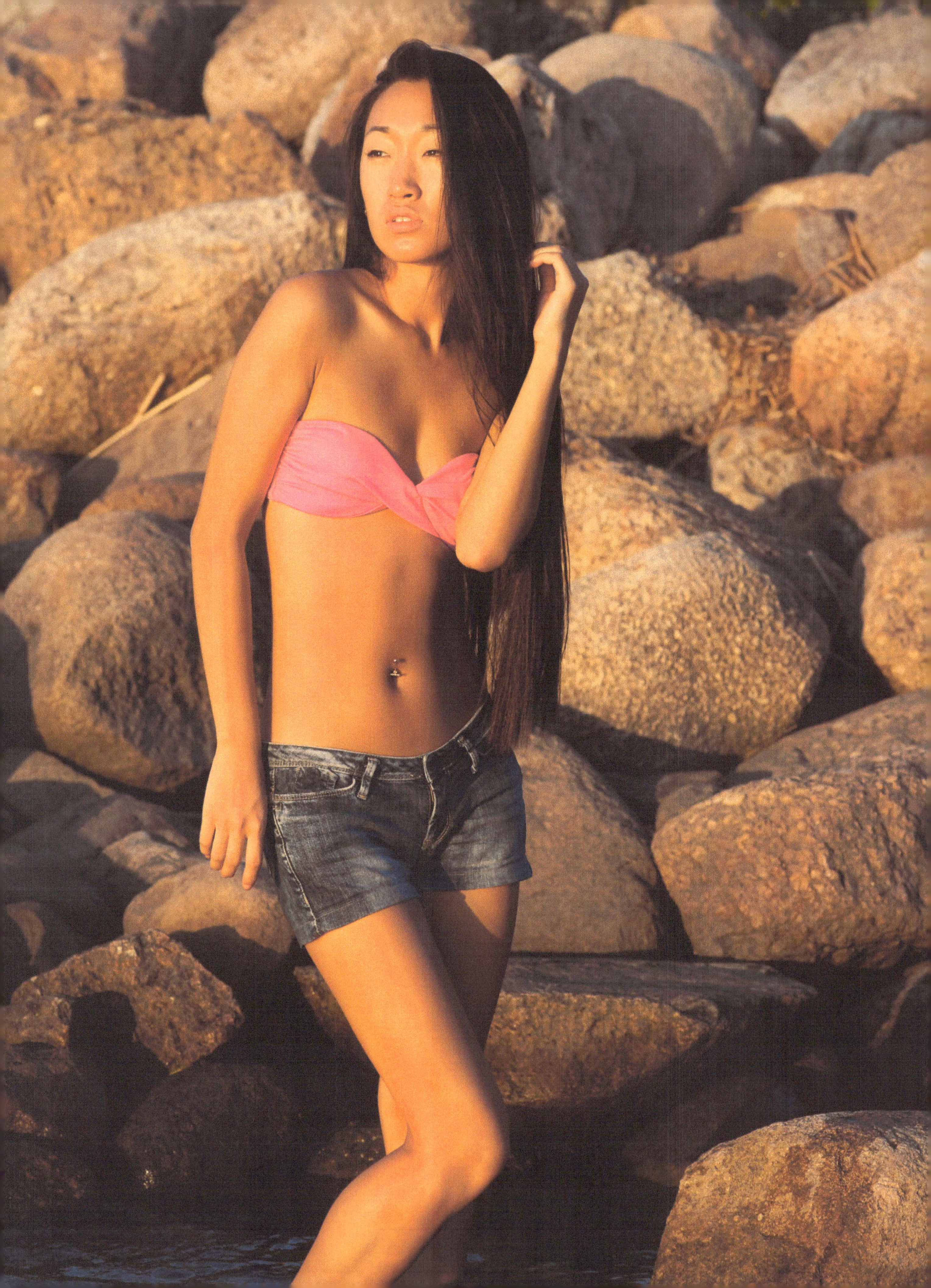

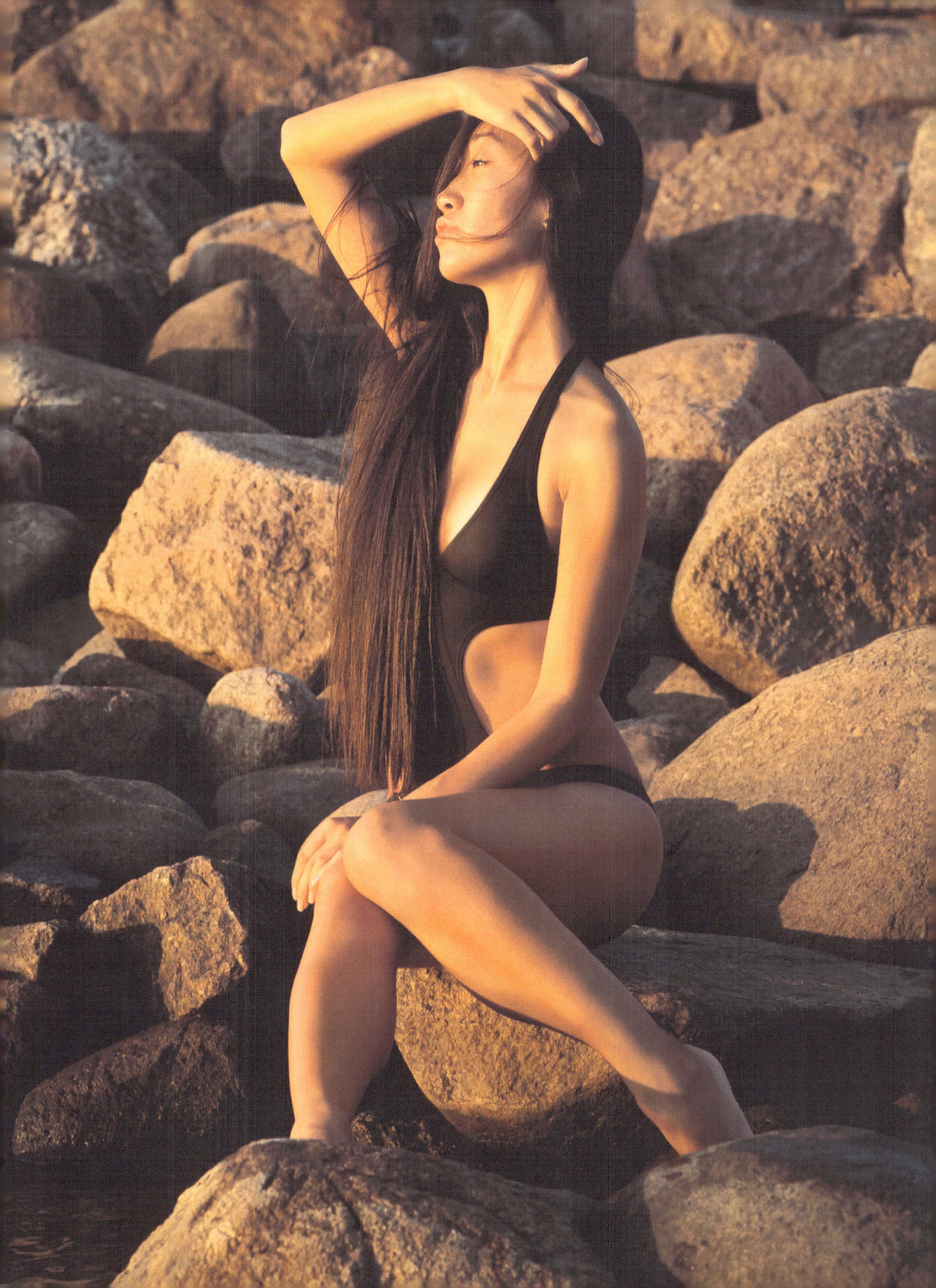

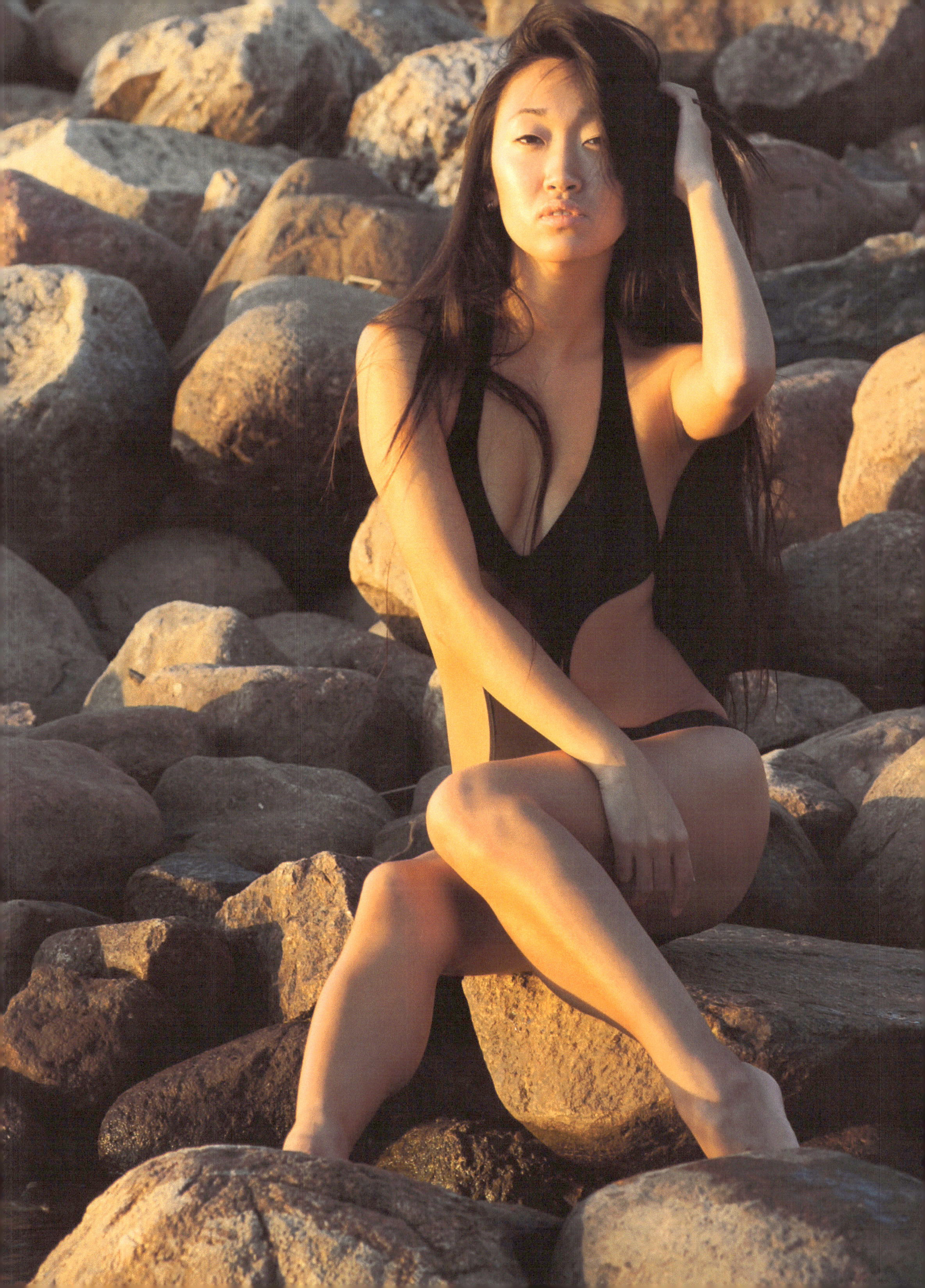

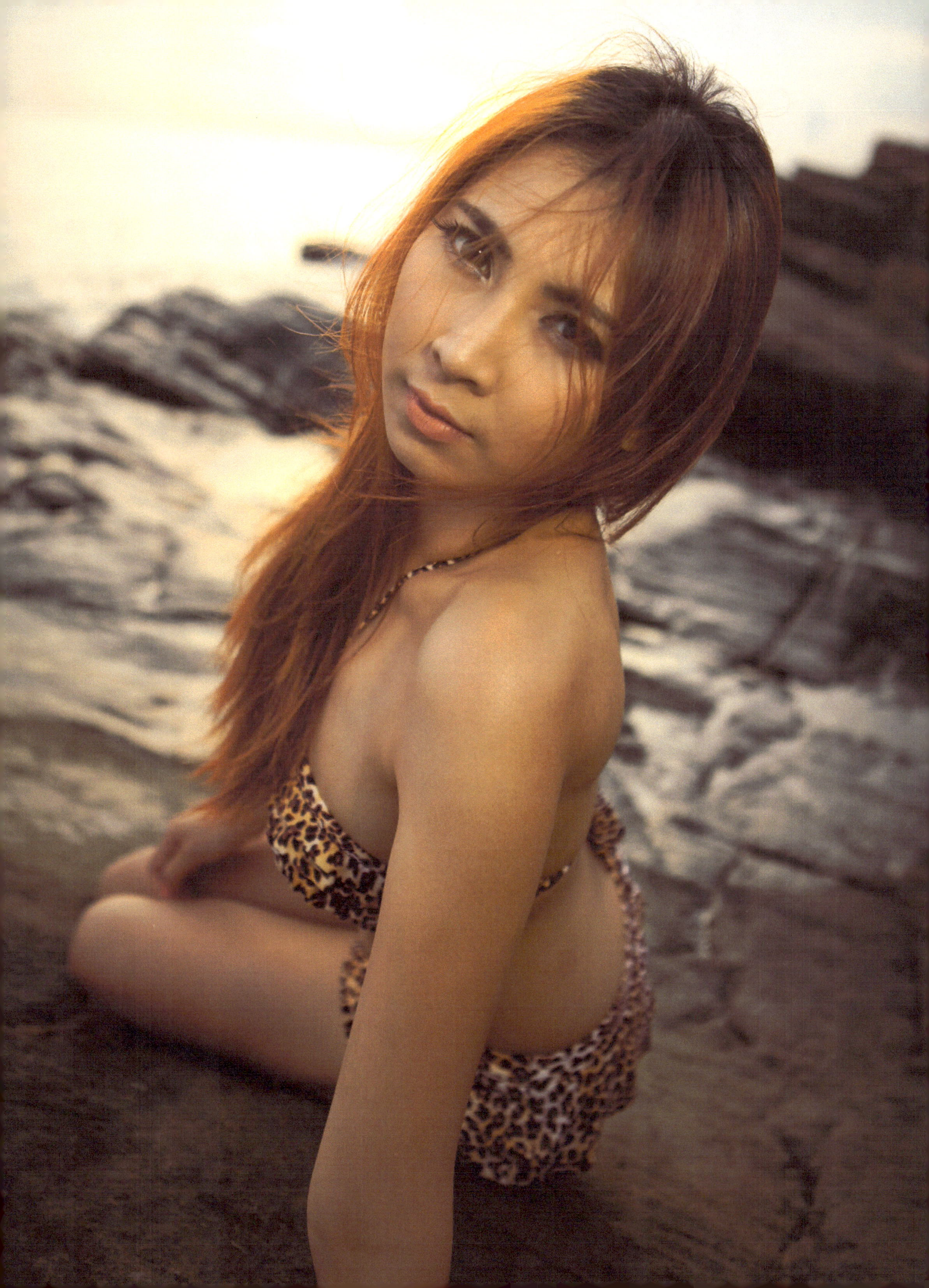

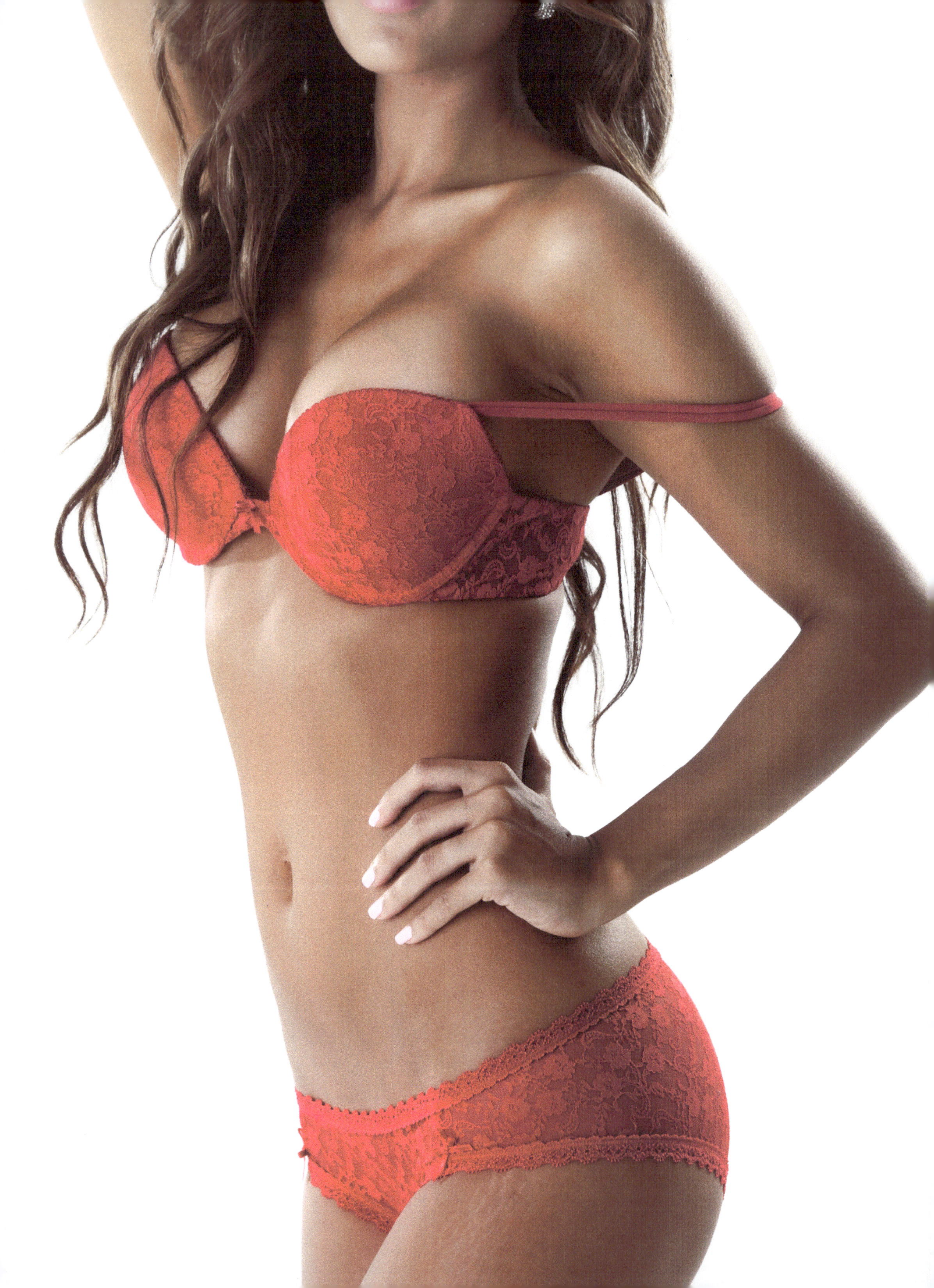

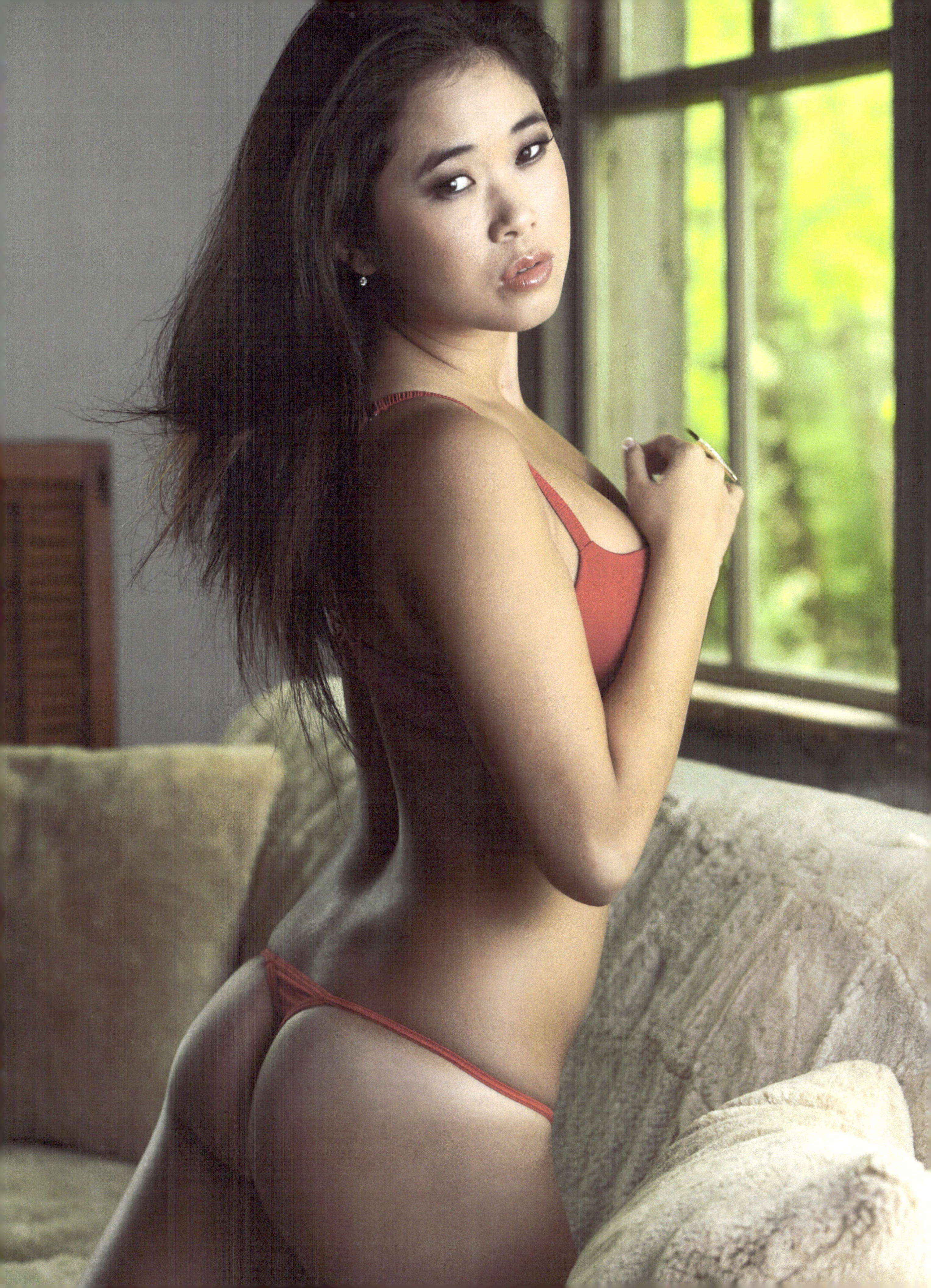

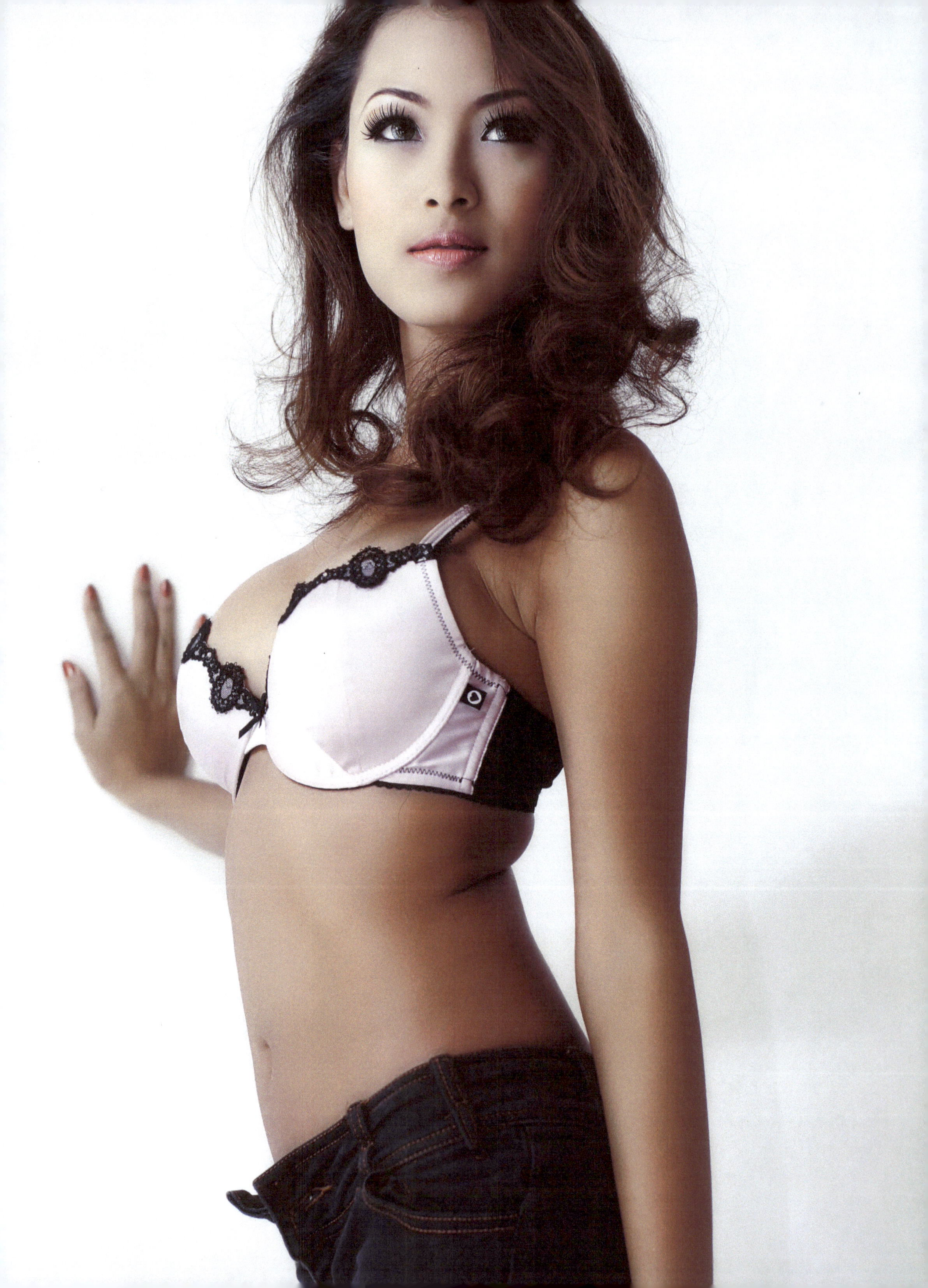

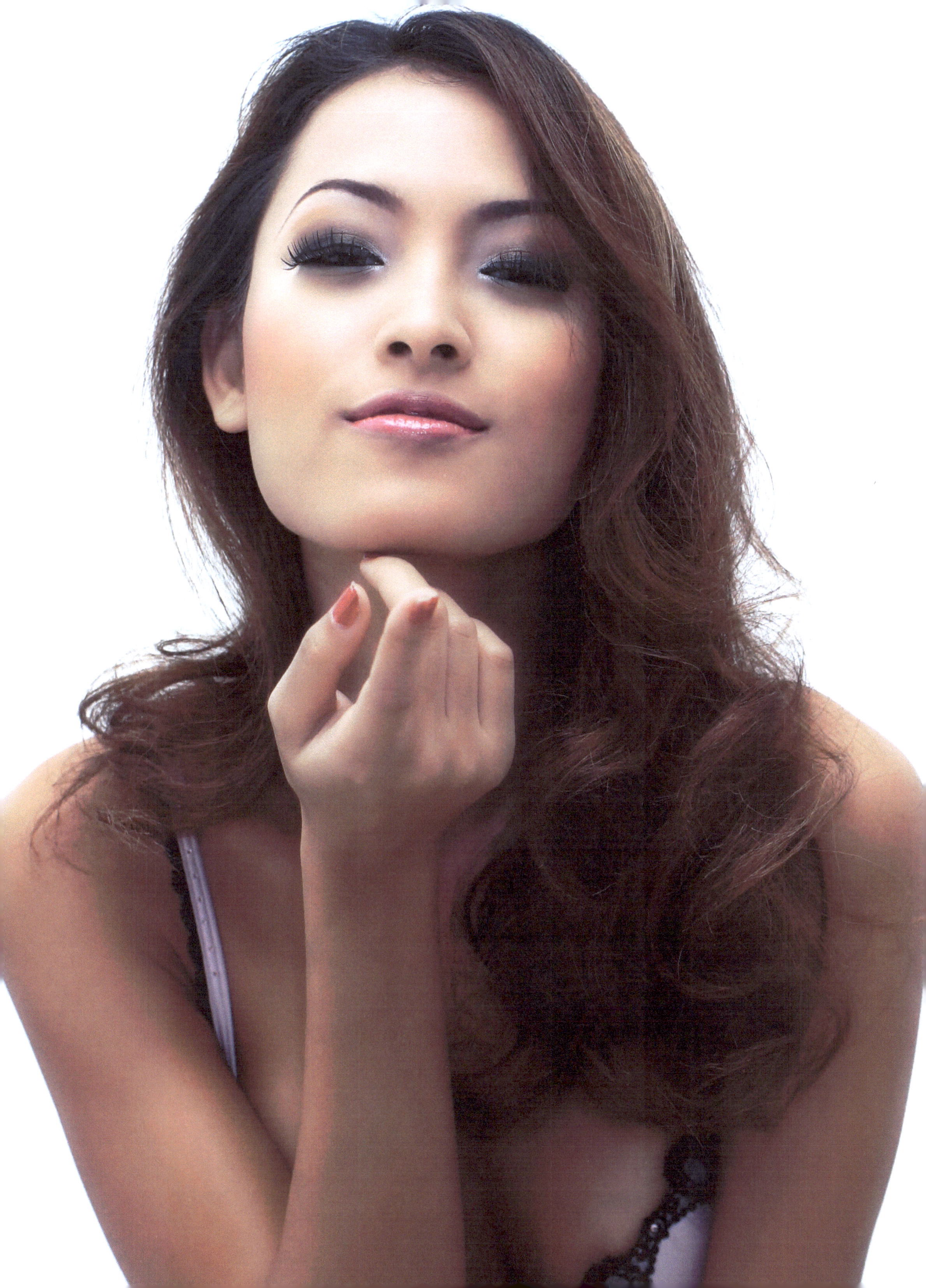

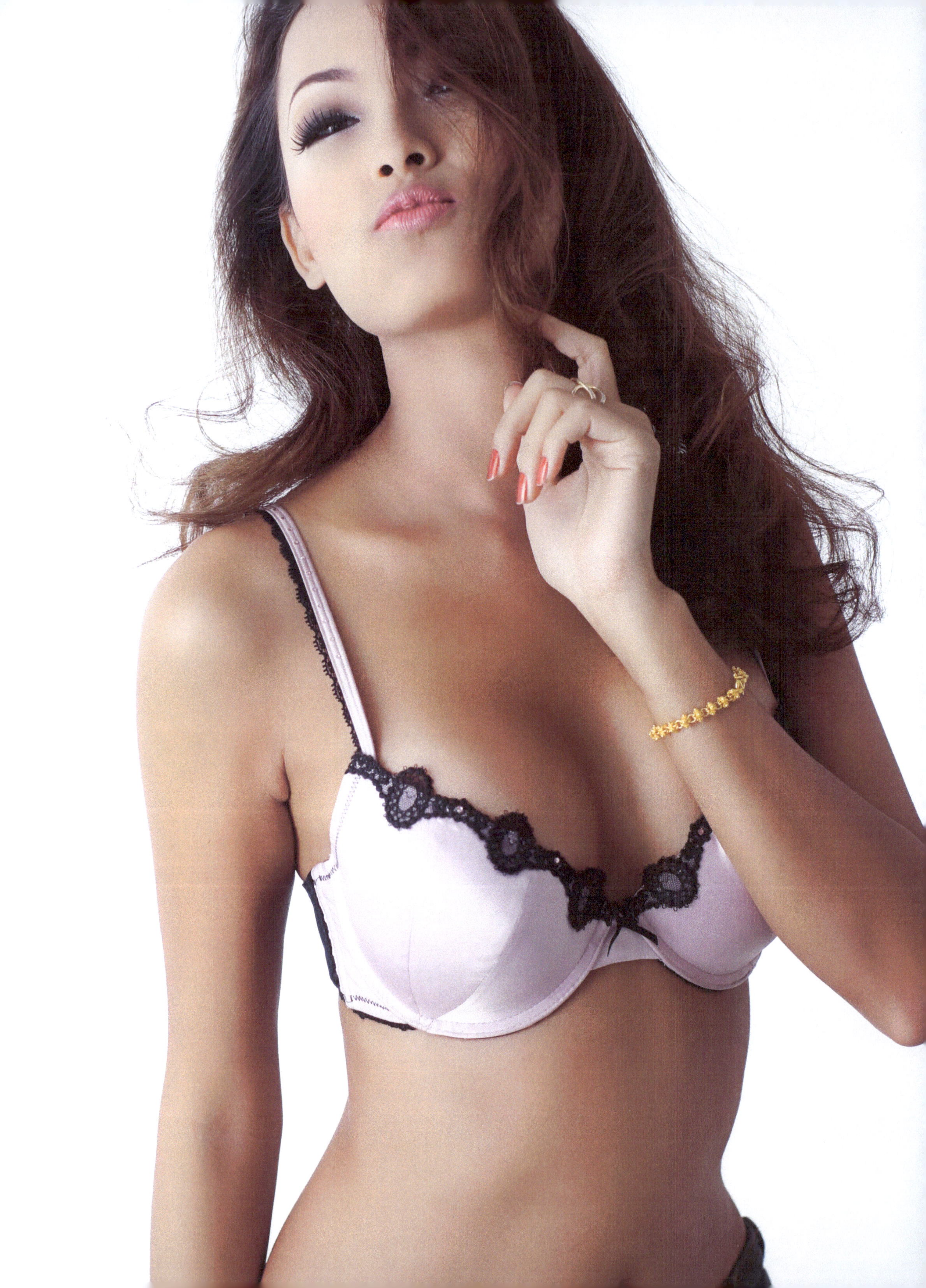

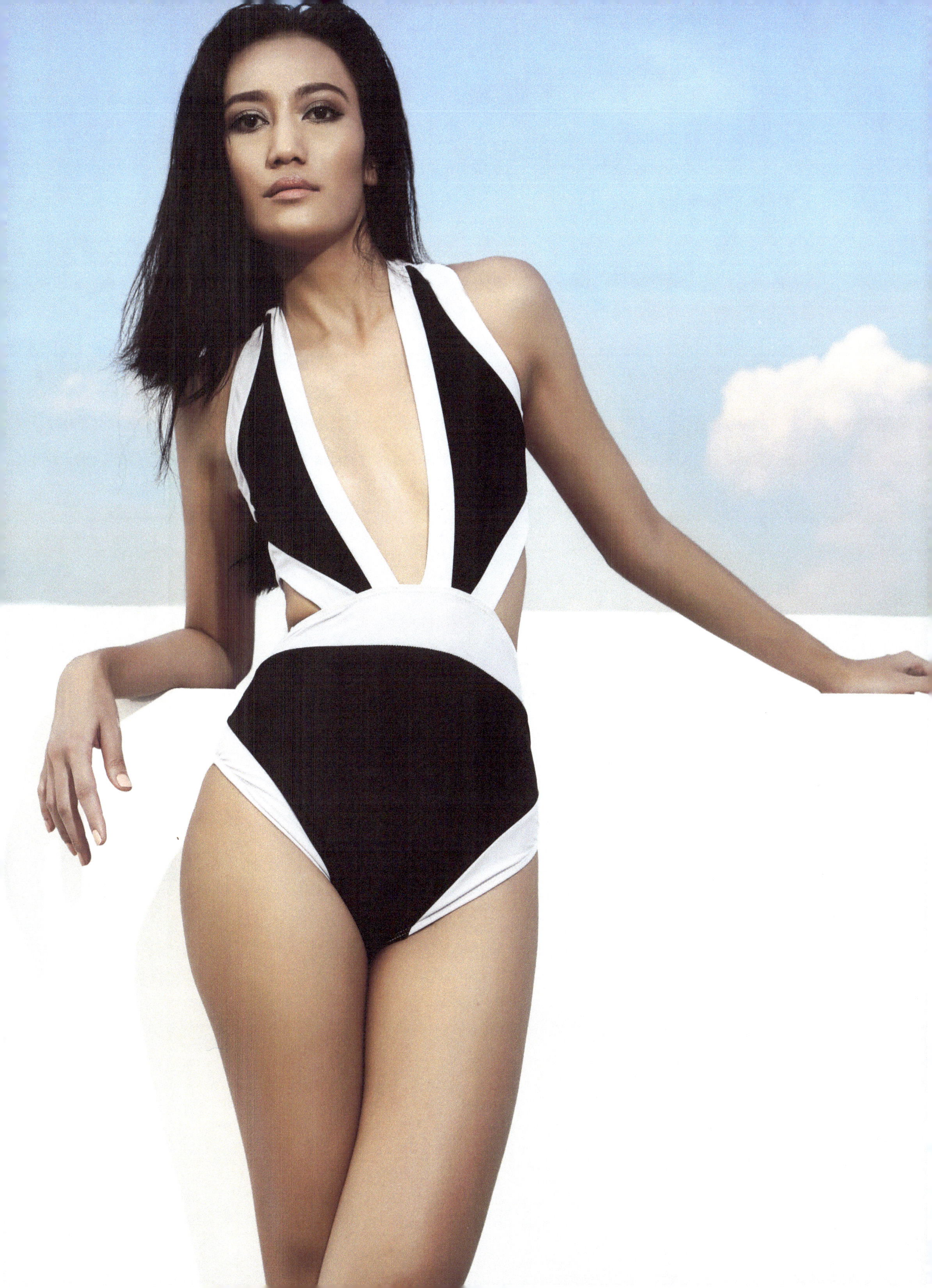

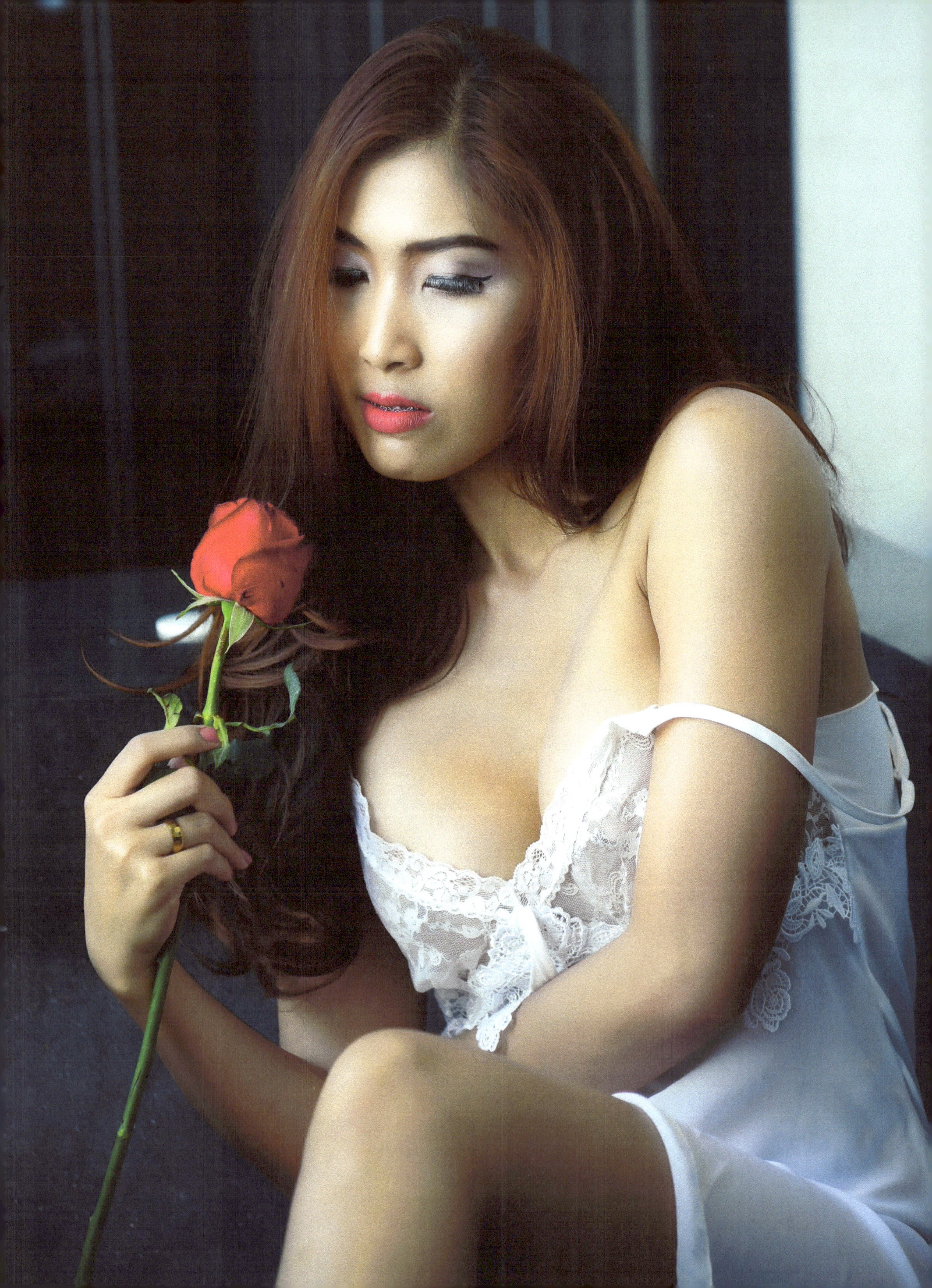

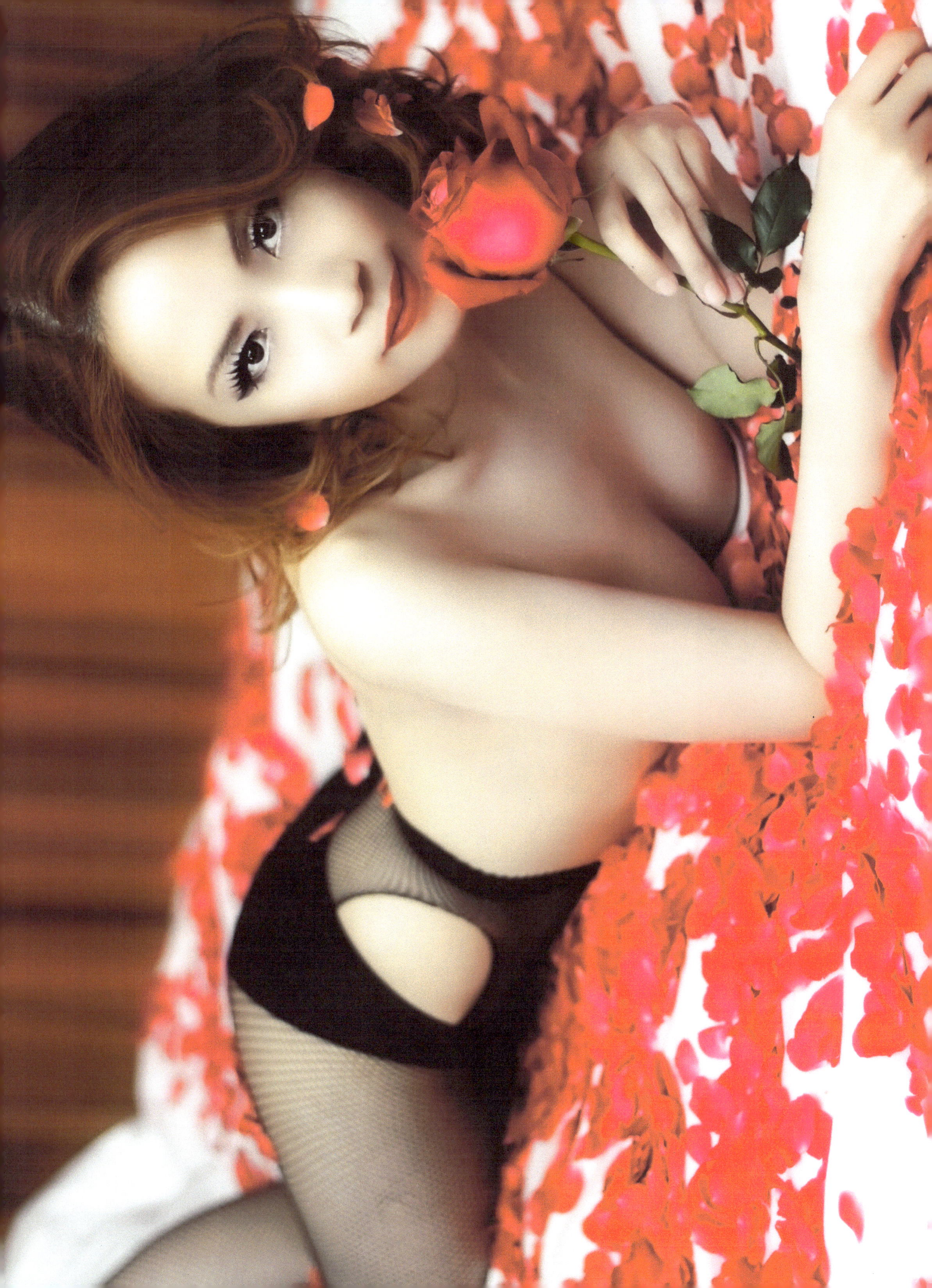

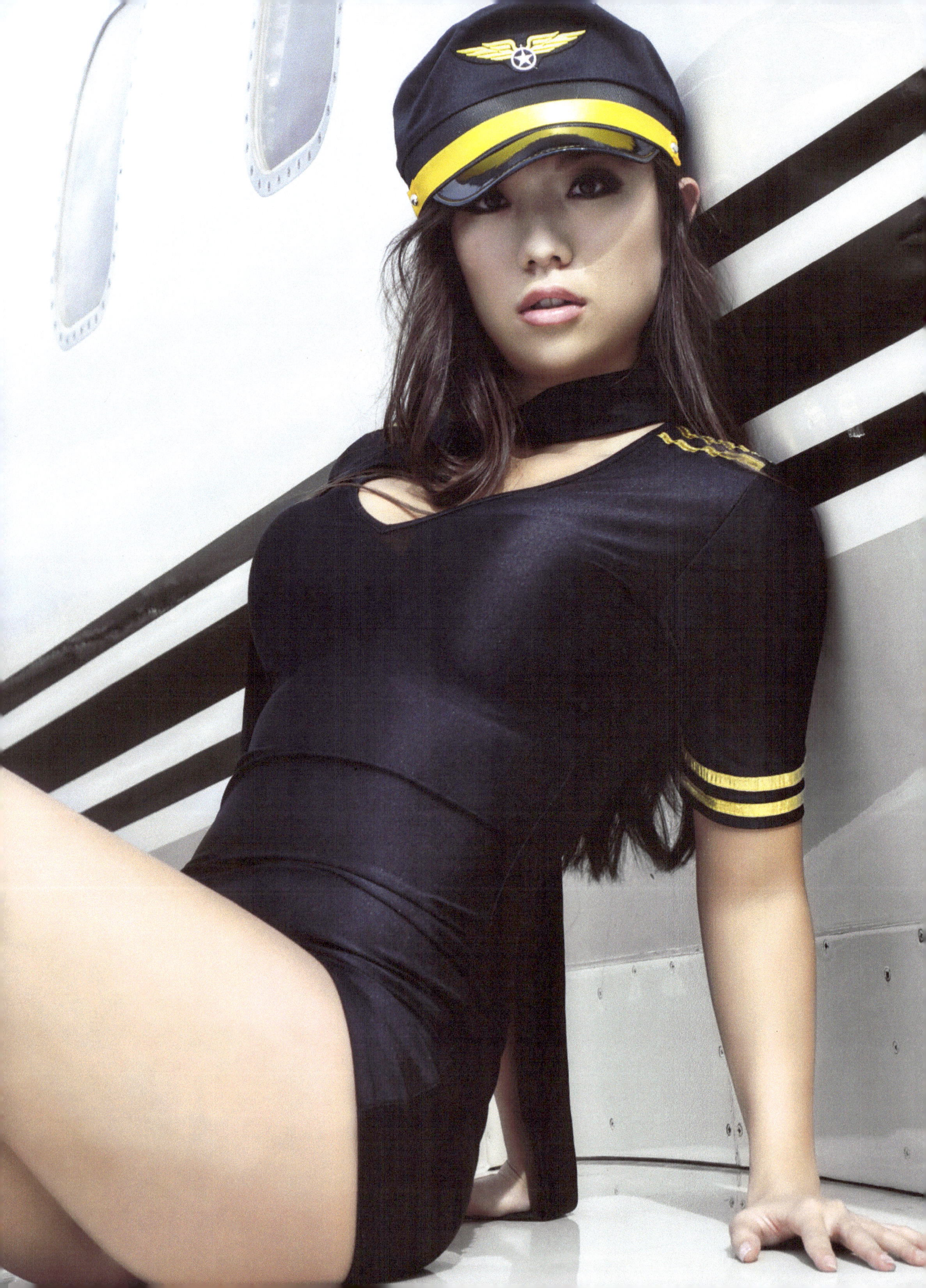

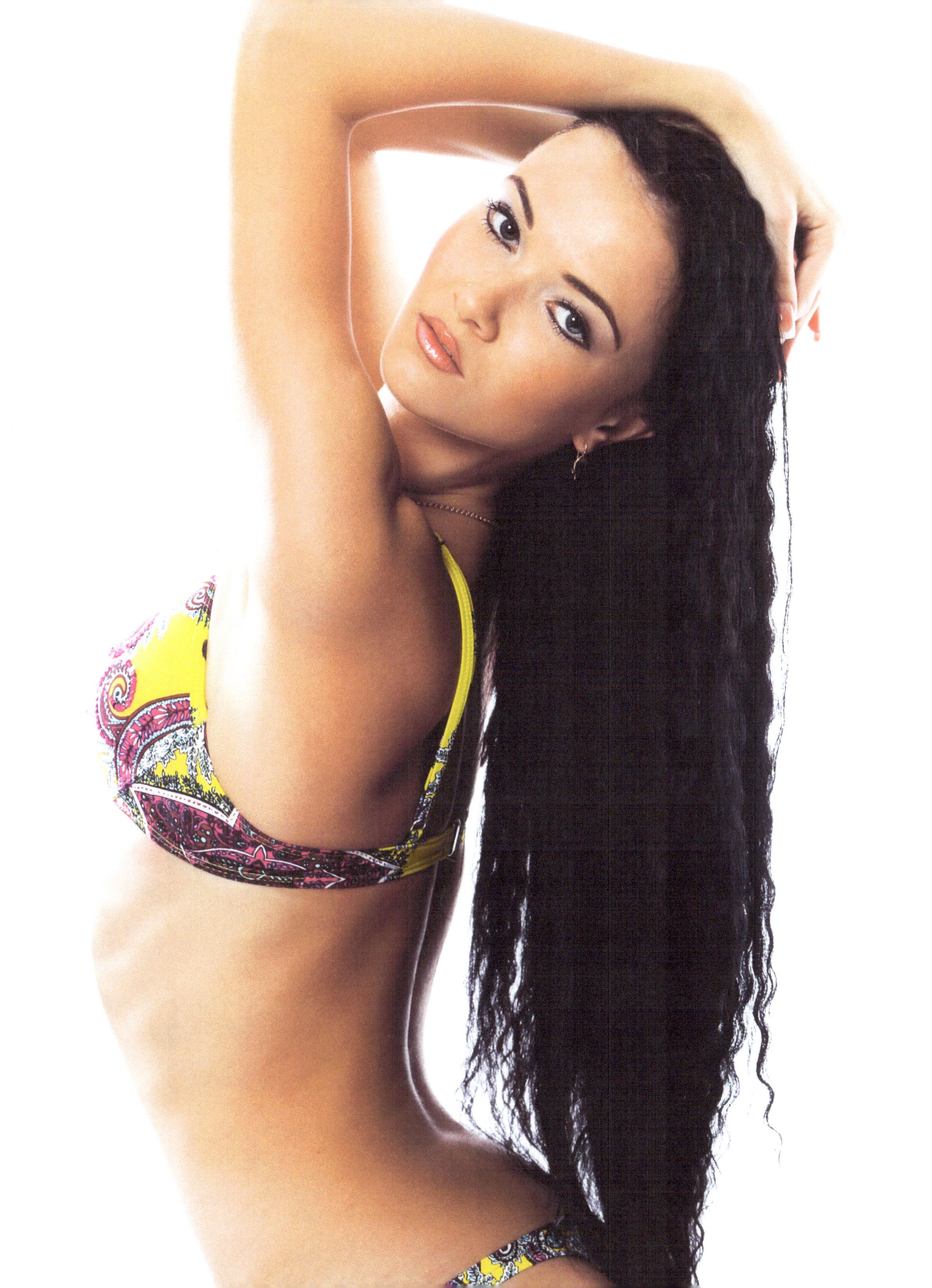

www.ingramcontent.com/pod-product-compliance
Lightning Source LLC
Chambersburg PA
CBHW050423180526
45159CB00005B/2387
* 9 7 8 1 5 3 9 1 0 0 6 4 5 *